Created and Written by
Shameeka Browne

Illustrated by Reggie Byers

Title: Queen of 24
Author: Shameeka Browne

Copyright © 2025 by Shameeka Browne
All rights reserved. No part of this book may be reproduced or transmitted in any form or by any means, electronic mechanical, including photo copying and image scanning, or information storage and retrieval systems without the written permission of the publisher and author of this book.

Library of Congress Control Number: 2025914712
ISBN: 9781953121059

Categories: Children's Fiction | Inspirational | STEM Education
Editor: Dana Fluder

Contact the Author at: info@mathisallaroundus.org
www.mathisallaroundus.org

Hello Mathematicians,

This book is dedicated to students everywhere, with the hope that you will see math all around you and find joy in exploring it.

May each page inspire your curiosity and love for learning.

Shameeka Browne

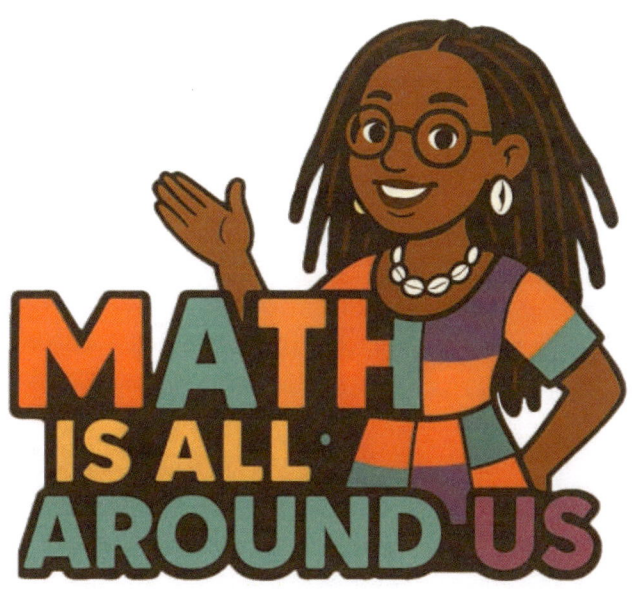

Foreword
by Robert Sun, Inventor of the 24® Game

When I first created the 24 game more than three decades ago, I never imagined it would spark a movement—a quiet revolution in how young people think about mathematics. I believed then, as I do now, that math is not just a subject in school but a universal language that helps us understand ourselves and the world around us. Through numbers, patterns, and the rhythm of problem-solving, students could come to see not only their intellect but also their potential.

Queen of 24 is a story that brings this vision to life in the most inspiring way. In these pages, you'll meet a young woman who discovers something extraordinary: that greatness isn't about where you start but how far you're willing to go. With every tap of the card, every moment of hesitation, and every comeback after doubt, she embodies what the 24 game teaches — grit, curiosity, and the joy of mastery.

This book is more than a personal journey. It is a powerful reminder of what happens when a child finds her spark. Shameeka Browne writes with honesty and heart, and her story reminds us that math does not reside only in textbooks or classrooms. It lives in street signs, cereal boxes, football jerseys, and field trips—even in our dreams. What makes her story so special is how it illustrates a profound truth: when students have the right tools, are encouraged, and step up to challenges, they don't just learn math—they *become* mathematicians.

As an immigrant child of a single mother growing up on the streets of West Philadelphia, I understand the feeling of not belonging, of looking around a room and wondering if you have a place there. Shameeka used the 24® game to build cumulative confidence and to help her find her place. Her courage—fueled by prayer, perseverance, and purpose—transforms her into something more than a competitor. She becomes a role model.

And if you've ever doubted whether you're "a math person," let this story show you that you already are.

I am honored that the 24 game could be part of Shameeka's journey, and I am even more honored to witness how her voice—and her vision—are now part of a new chapter in the 24 game legacy.

To the next Queen or King of 24 reading this: your journey is just beginning. And I can't wait to see where it takes you.

– Robert Sun
Inventor of the 24 game and First In Math

The Queen of 24 - that's **me**! This is my story.

As the numbers on the cards swam before my eyes, my brain went blank. No words would come out of my mouth.

I tapped a card but couldn't speak.
Penalty.

I took a deep breath.

How did I get here? Let me tell you...

As a middle schooler, I wasn't always interested in numbers or math. Until the day I first met 24. It happened at General Louis Wagner Middle School in Philadelphia, the city where I was born and raised.

 The game of 24 is simple but exciting: To win, you have to accumulate the highest score by being the first to solve the playing cards.

Each card has four numbers on it. You tap the card with three fingers to solve it. Using each number only once, you arrive at 24 by applying addition, subtraction, multiplication, or division to the four numbers. You have three seconds to explain your answer. Penalty flags are given for incorrect or delayed responses. To win, you have to think fast.

I discovered that 24 is the most amazing number! I was born on May 24th. Even the digits of my birth year - 1, 9, 8, and 3 - can be arranged to make 24. Check it out:

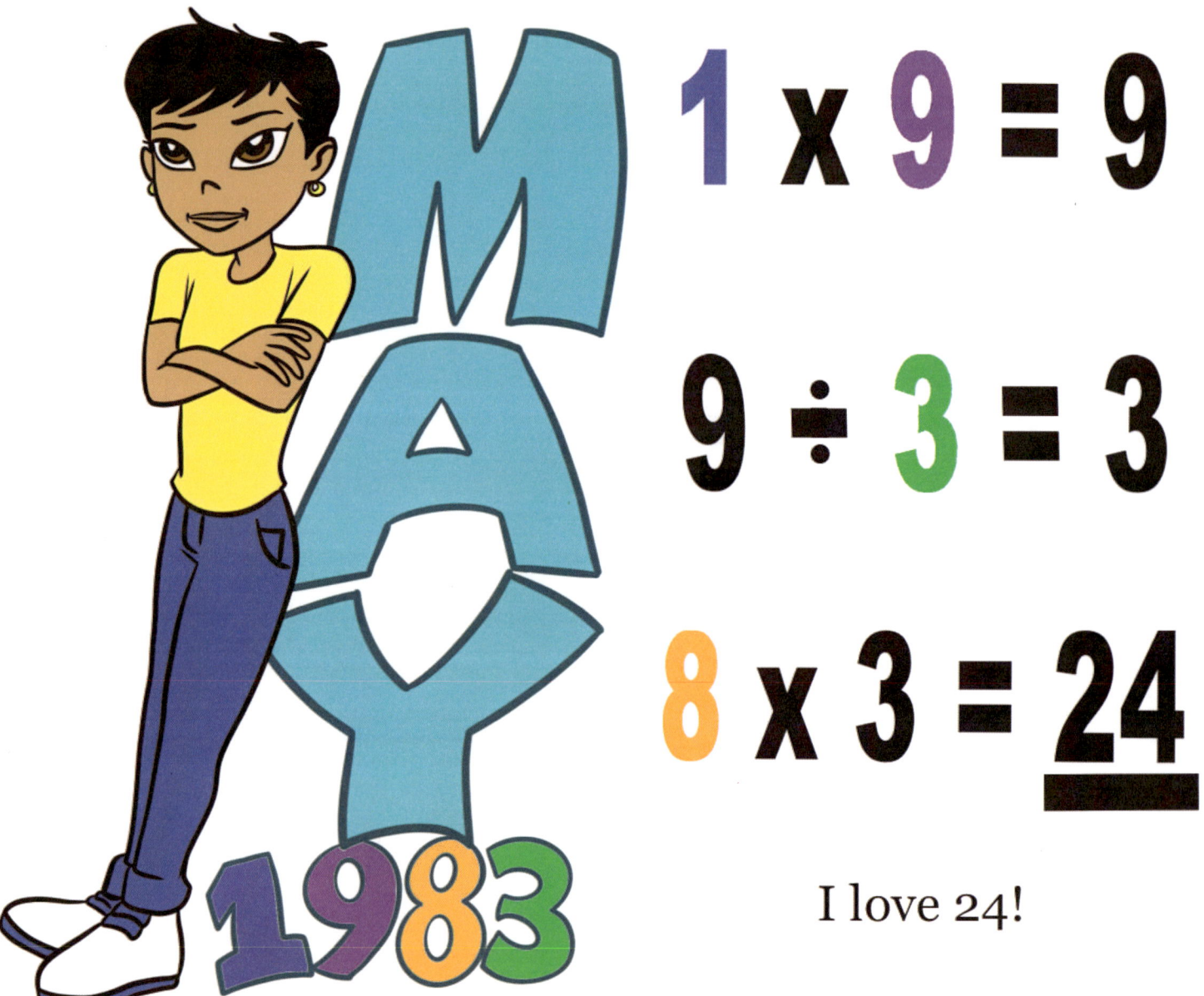

1 x 9 = 9

9 ÷ 3 = 3

8 x 3 = <u>24</u>

I love 24!

I practiced. And practiced. And practiced.
Before long, I started to notice numbers all around me, and guess what I did with them? I made 24. I made 24 with the street addresses I passed as I walked home from school.
I made 24 with the license plate numbers.

I made 24 while training at Vita Saana African Martial Arts classes. I made 24 from the numbers I read from the cereal box while eating breakfast before school.

I made 24 from the football jerseys as I cheered from the sideline.
GO RAIDERS!

I made 24 as I devoured my favorite meal that only my mom has mastered, stew chicken and dumplings.

I made 24 while I got my hair braided at the African braiding salon.

The numbers I saw in my dreams? You guessed it - 24! Can you make 24?

Then I learned about the Platinum Level of 24. This was next-level math! To win, I had to use squares, cubes, and roots - plus fractions and decimals. I loved the challenge. I discovered cool number patterns, and before I knew it, I was a math whiz in my class!

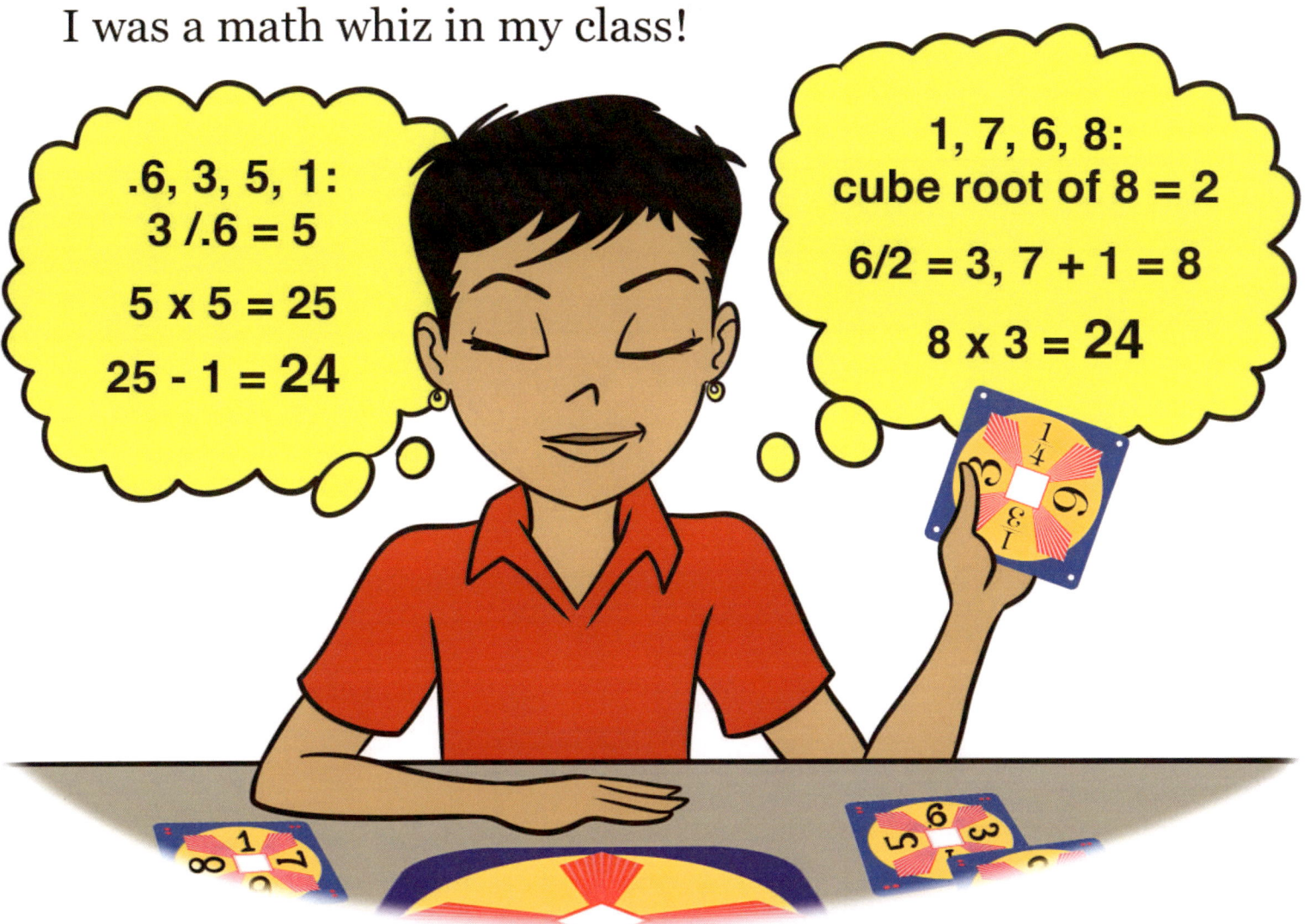

.6, 3, 5, 1:
3 /.6 = 5
5 x 5 = 25
25 - 1 = 24

1, 7, 6, 8:
cube root of 8 = 2
6/2 = 3, 7 + 1 = 8
8 x 3 = 24

How many different ways can you make 24?

With practice, I got faster and faster.
Soon, I beat every student in my class.
Then I beat every student in my school.
Then I defeated every student in my entire school district.

I became the Queen of 24.

My friend and I advanced to the state-wide 24 competition! It happened to be on the same day as my eighth grade end-of-the-year field trip. Being the Queen of 24 sometimes required sacrifice, but I was dedicated. So I traveled with my friend and our teachers to the Franklin Institute Museum to participate. I was excited - but also nervous.

Help! Can you make 24?

When I arrived, I saw so many students from school districts across Pennsylvania. For the first time, I was competing against kids who did not look like me. The room buzzed with excitement, and suddenly, I felt different. I began to doubt myself.

The 24 coordinator reminded us of the game rules.

Then, the first round began.

"You don't belong here," whispered a voice in my head. "Look around - these kids probably attend expensive math camps all summer."

I stared at the card, but the numbers blurred together. Was I really going to embarrass myself in front of everyone?

I froze.

My brain went blank. The numbers on the cards swam before my eyes. No words would come out of my mouth.

I tapped another card but couldn't speak.
Penalty.

I tapped another card but still said nothing.
Penalty.

One more mistake, and I'd be eliminated.
Time was running out.

My stomach tightened as I looked around the room. Would they laugh if I made a mistake?

I closed my eyes for a second and remembered my bedroom wall covered in practice problems.
All those late nights. I belonged here as much as anyone.

The familiar rush of numbers started flowing through my brain again. 8, 3, 4, 2... I could see the patterns connecting like a map only I could read.

I took a deep breath. I looked up to God for help...

Then, something inside me clicked.
I was the Queen of 24 - and I was back.
I tapped the Platinum Level cards, solving them before my opponents could react.
Faster, faster, faster.

With each correct answer, a little voice inside grew stronger: *"You've got this. You ARE the Queen of 24! You can do all things through Christ who strengthens you!"*

One after another, I climbed the scoreboard.
I advanced to the second round. Then, the third round leading up to the semifinals.

I fought hard. At the end of the competition, I took fifth place out of all the students in Pennsylvania! Even though I hadn't always loved math, and even though I didn't look like the other kids competing, I had overcome through practice and perseverance.
I was proud of my achievement.

At eighth grade move-up day, the principal called my name. She recognized me for my hard work and achievement - not just in academics, but also in the Game of 24. My friends cheered.
I smiled, standing tall.

Middle school was the time I fell in love with 24.
I fell in love with math! **And you can, too.**

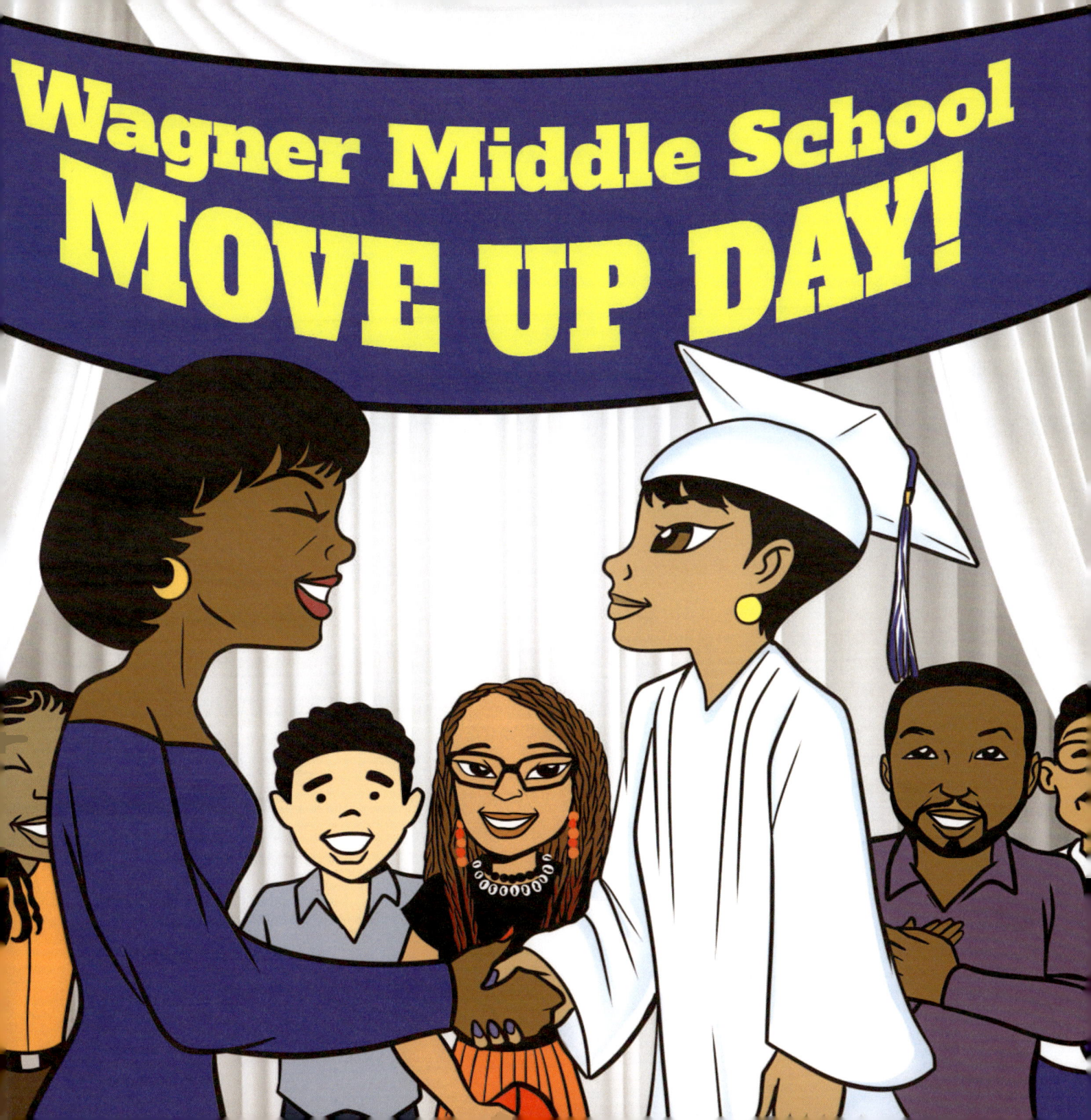

Look for four numbers around you.
Can you utilize math to make 24?

Pro tip: Start with memorizing the factors of 24 - like 1 x 24, 2 x 12, 3 x 8, or 4 x 6.
Or discover fun combinations like 30 - 6, 15 + 9, or 21 + 3. When you reach the Platinum level, you can start to memorize squares, cubes, square roots, and cube roots.

Go ahead - give it a try!
You, too, can be the Queen (or King!) of 24!

A Reflection from the Author

Thank you for reading *Queen of 24*, my very first children's book.

I fell in love with reading in elementary school and discovered my love for math in middle school. I was blessed to have amazing teachers who saw my potential. They challenged me with new books and rich math experiences, and because of their encouragement, I began to thrive. Even today, I carry a book or two in my bag, always ready to read whenever I get the chance. And no matter where I go, I find joy in spotting numbers in my community and figuring out how to make 24.

I never imagined I would become an author. For over three years, I wrestled with imposter syndrome. I often wondered, *Is my story good enough? is it deep enough? Will it make a difference?* But I pushed through those doubts, and now I hope to inspire you to do the same.

Take a moment to reflect:
Have you fallen in love with something yet?
An activity, subject, or talent? What is it?

What passions would you like to grow into something more?

Can you remember a time when you doubted yourself? What helped you move forward?

It's also important to be kind - especially during competitions. Everyone handles losing differently. Some people bounce back right away, while others need time and space to regroup.

What are some healthy values or mindsets to have when it comes to competition?

How do you encourage others after a tough moment? How do you encourage yourself?

Being a Queen - or King - of something meaningful takes sacrifice. But dream big and never lose hope. With hard work, kindness, and courage, there is nothing you cannot achieve.
There is greatness in you.
You are enough.

With love and belief,
Shameeka Browne

The greatest honor a teacher can get happens when your student becomes your colleague. I am so proud of the incredible path Shameeka has taken to inspire young minds as a math teacher and now as an author! Writing a children's book about math is such a creative and impactful endeavor; a beautiful way to make the subject come alive for young learners.

You have learned that teaching is not about knowing all the correct answers. Teaching is about knowing the right questions to ask. It is about growing intelligence by creating an enriched environment where students seek to solve problems in collaboration with other learners. It is about helping students to make connections between learning and life or as you put it "math all around us."

Your dedication to education and your passion for sharing knowledge shine through, and I have no doubt that your book will spark curiosity and joy in countless children. It is a privilege to see you grow as a teacher and storyteller and to have known you as both my student and colleague.

Congratulations on this wonderful accomplishment! I cannot wait to read your book and see the magic you have created. I am so proud of you!

Your eighth-grade teacher,
Gary Plummer

Math Glossary

Cube – The product of a number multiplied by itself three times.
Example: 2 × 2 × 2 = 8.

Cube Root – A number that, when cubed, results in the original number.
Example: The cube root of 27 is 3.

Factor – A number that divides evenly into another number.
Example: The factors of 24 are 1, 2, 3, 4, 6, 8, 12, and 24.

Product – The result of multiplying two or more numbers. Example: 6 × 4 = 24.

Quotient – The result of division.
Example: 48 ÷ 2 = 24.

Square – The product of a number multiplied by itself.
Example: 4 × 4 = 16.

Square Root – A number that, when squared, gives the original number. Example: The square root of 9 is 3.

Sum – The total when two or more numbers are added together. Example: 12 + 12 = 24.

Visit www.mathisallaroundus.org or scan the QR code below to access free downloads of additional journal space and math activities.

www.ingramcontent.com/pod-product-compliance
Lightning Source LLC
Chambersburg PA
CBRC090910230426
43673CB00017B/424